MORE

23 Heartwarming

GOSPEL

and Toe-tapping Songs

TRUTH

for Adult Choir

ARRANGED BY TOM FETTKE

Lillenas PUBLISHING COMPANY

KANSAS CITY, MO 64141

Contents

When the Lamb Becomes the Light

Words and Music by
REGIE HAMM and
JOEL LINDSEY
Arr. by Tom Fettke

There will be no weep - ing, no more sor - row, no more night When the Lamb be - comes the Light.

CD: 3

Freely

10

Those Good Old Gospel Songs

Good Old Gospel Songs
with optional congregational participation on
Wonderful Grace of Jesus
My Savior's Love
Blessed Be the Name

Arr. by Tom Fettke

*"Good Old Gospel Songs" (Squire E. Parsons, Jr.)

There's_____ some-thing a - bout_____ a good old gos - pel song,_____

That brings joy to the heart_____ when

CD: 7

good old gos - pel song._____

*"Wonderful Grace of Jesus" (Haldor Lillenas)
Gospel two-beat feel
Congregation may join / Harmony optional for choir

Won - der-ful grace of Je - sus, Great - er than all my

Straight eighths

sin-_____ How shall my tongue de - scribe it?

CD: 9

*"My Savior's Love" (Charles H. Gabriel)

*"Blessed Be the Name" (Ralph E. Hudson)

some-thing a - bout,

117

Some- thing a - bout_____ a good old gos - pel song._____

Though Your Sins Be As Scarlet

Words and Music by
WAYNE GOODINE
Arr. by Tom Fettke

CD: 15

crim - son, They shall be_____ white as snow.

*"Wonder Working Power" (Oliver Cooke/Tom Fettke)

a tempo
mf *Solo (or ladies unison)*

I know a fount where sins are washed a - way,_____

I know a place where night is turned to day;_____

Let All the World Cry "Holy"

A cappella

Words and Music by
MOSIE LISTER
Arr. by Tom Fettke

Victory Shall Be Mine

Words and Music by
NANCY HARMON
Arr. by Tom Fettke
and Russell Mauldin

There's a bat-tle_____ we're en-gaged in,

There's a goal line_____ we must cross.

There's a weight_____ that must be lift - ed,

There's a tro - phy_____ to be won.

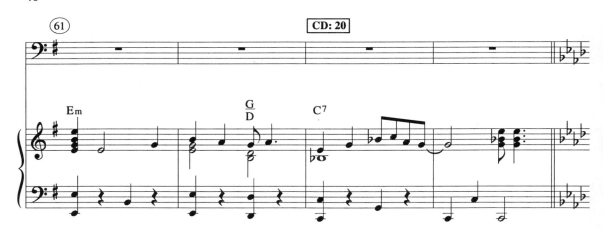

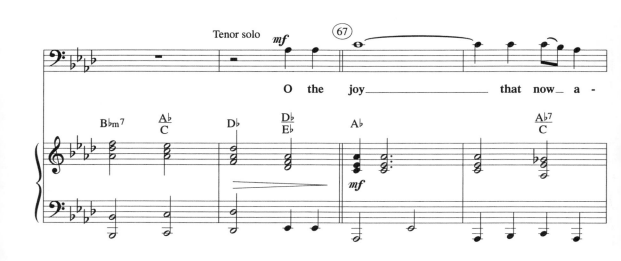

O the joy_____ that now_ a-

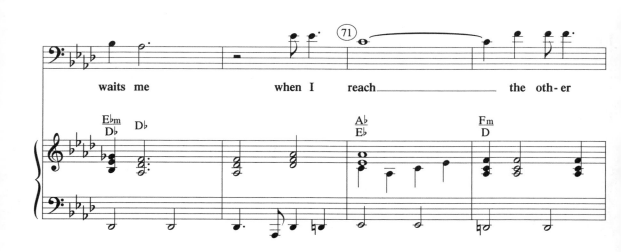

waits me when I reach_____ the oth- er

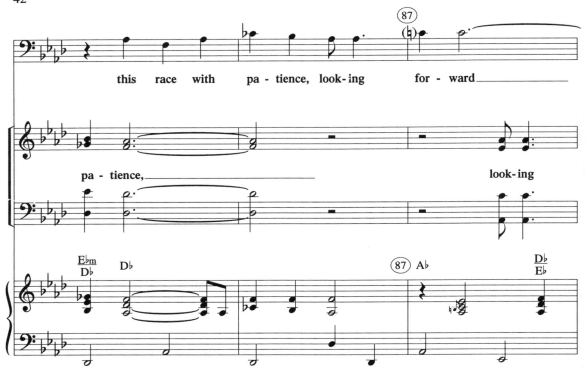

this race with pa - tience, look- ing for - ward_____

pa - tience,_____ look- ing

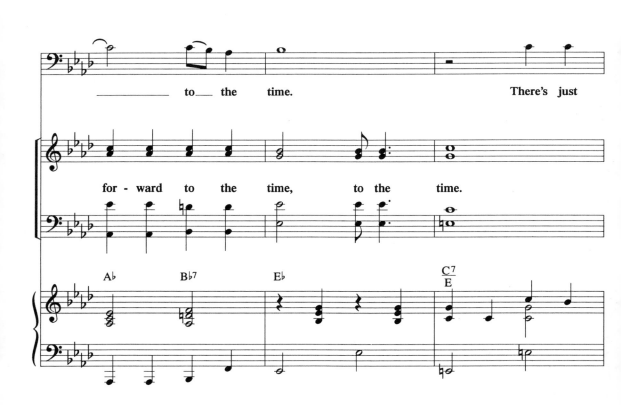

_____ to__ the time. There's just

for - ward to the time, to the time.

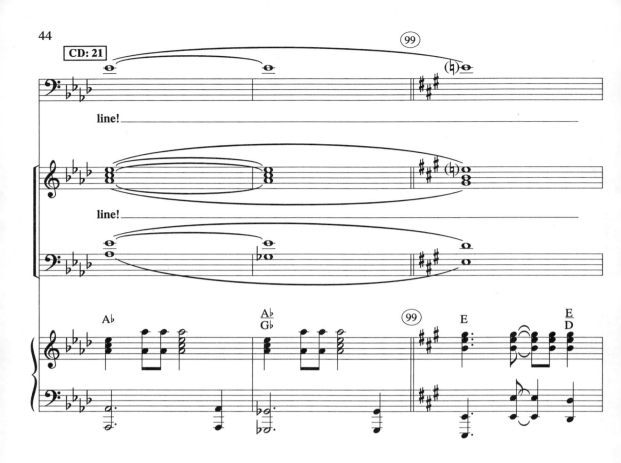

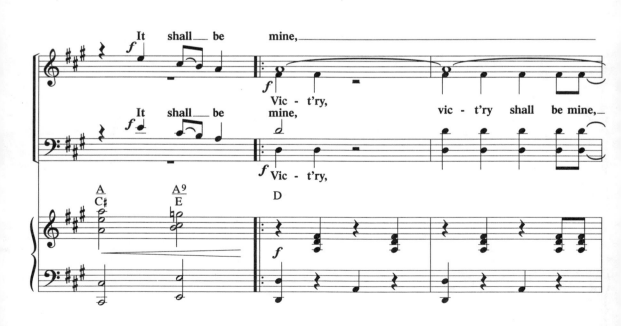

He Came to Me

with

He Giveth More Grace

Words and Music by
SQUIRE E. PARSONS, JR.
Arr. by Tom Fettke

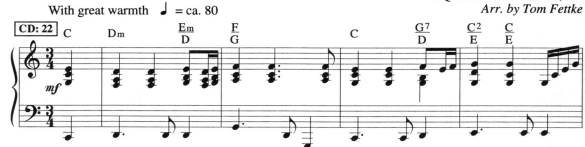

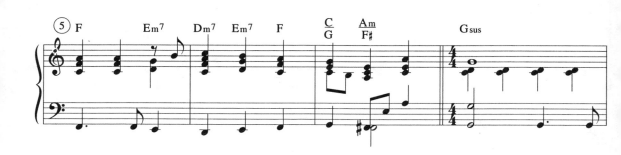

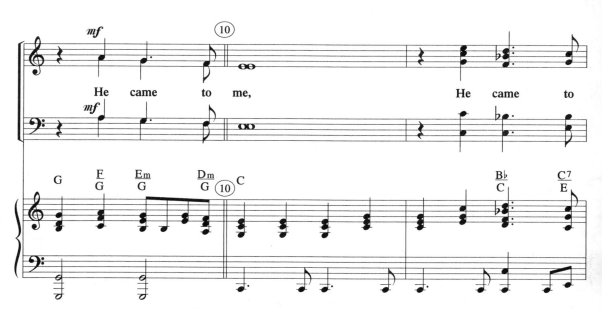

He came to me, He came to

ry; When I could not come to where He was, He came to

me.

me, He came to me. He came to

CD: 23

me when I was bound in chains of sin,

He came to me when I pos-sessed no hope with-in; He picked me up and drew me gen-tly to His side, And now to-

52

day in His sweet love I now a - bide.

*"He Giveth More Grace" (Flint/Mitchell)

Unison

His love has no lim - it; His

grace has no mea - sure; His pow'r has no

54

58

He's All I Need

A cappella

Traditional and
KEN BIBLE

Traditional
Arr. by Tom Fettke

59

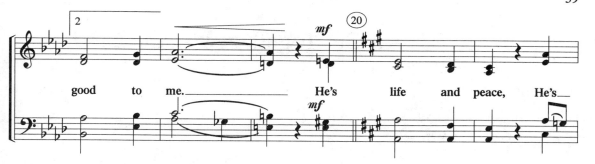

When We All Get Together with the Lord

Traditional

Traditional
Arr. by Tom Fettke
and Russell Mauldin

Well,___ God has no fav-'rites, He just loves us all the same. His Son died to save us and to keep us in His name. And soon we'll rise to meet Him and for -

Wedding Music

with

Celebrate His Coming

Words and Music by
KIRK TALLEY
and **PHIL CROSS**
Arr. by Tom Fettke

Smoothly, heavenly ♩ = ca. 100

CD: 31

*"Soon and Very Soon" (Andrae Crouch)

N.C.

mp

mf

mf

Is that wed - ding mu - sic that I hear?

mf

D♭/A♭   G♭   D♭/A♭   A♭7   G♭/D♭

With anticipation

Is that wed - ding mu - sic I

D♭

All have been in-vit-ed to at-tend.

The bride is stand-ing read-y,

Wait-ing for the sig-nal, When the groom says, "Rise, my

*"Celebrate His Coming" (Josh McPheeters)

I'll Fly Away

with

We'll Understand It Better By and By

Words and Music by
ALBERT E. BRUMLEY
*Arr. by Tom Fettke
and Richard Kingsmore*

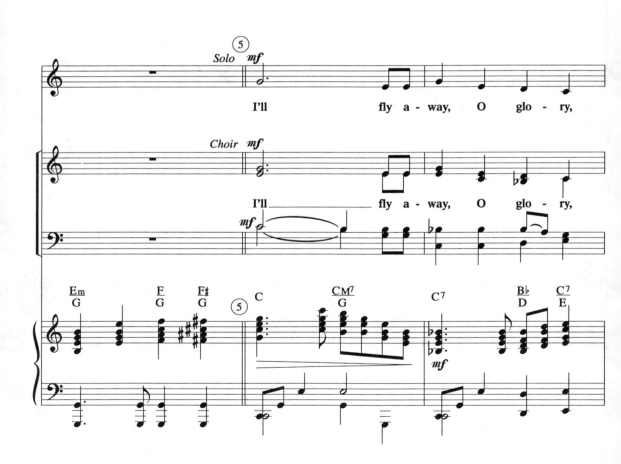

CD: 36

84

86

He'll Understand and Say, "Well Done"

LUCY E. CAMPBELL
and KEN BIBLE

LUCY E. CAMPBELL
Arr. by Tom Fettke

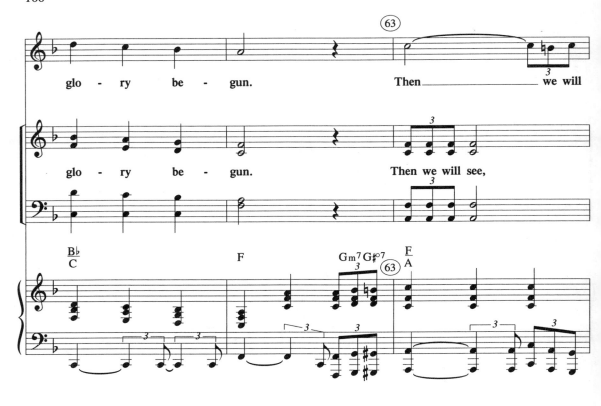

Let Me Touch Him

A cappella

Words and Music by
VEP ELLIS
Arr. by Tom Fettke

With warmth

mf

Let me touch Him, let me touch Je - sus, Let me

5

touch Him as He pass - es by; Then when

9

I shall reach out to oth - ers, They shall

13

know Him, they shall live and not die. O to

Raise the Roof

Words and Music by
JOEL LINDSEY and
ERNIE HAASE
Arr. by Tom Fettke
and Richard Kingsmore

Solo (female or male)

It was ru- mored that Je- sus had come To the ti- ny lit- tle town____ Ca- per- na- um.____

Here Comes the King

MOSIE LISTER and KEN BIBLE

MOSIE LISTER
Arr. by Tom Fettke

Here comes——— the King, Here comes——— the King! In

Coming Again

A cappella

Words and Music by
MOSIE LISTER
Arr. by Tom Fettke

1. Je - sus is com - ing; Je - sus is com - ing; Je - sus___ is com - ing, He's com - ing a - gain.
2. We'll rise to meet_ Him; We'll rise to meet_ Him; We'll rise___ to meet_ Him, He's com - ing a - gain.

3. We shall be like_ Him; We shall be like_ Him; We shall___ be like_ Him, He's com - ing a - gain. gain.

Out of His Great Love

Words and Music by
TERRY and BARBI FRANKLIN
Arr. by Tom Fettke
and Kyle Hill

With energy ♩ = ca. 140

CD: 55

1st time: all unison on melody (soprano part)
2nd time: parts *f*

Out of His great love He picked me____ up,

126

128

Out of His Great Love (*optional reprise)

Congregational participation optional

CD: 59

Out of His great love He picked me_ up, Set my feet on a stur - dy rock; Out of His great love I've learned the mean - ing_ of Sal - va - tion out of His great

*Use as an encore or heightened continuation of praise atmosphere. Accompaniment track is included on all track formats.